MORE QUESTIONS THAN ANSWERS?

MORE QUESTIONS THAN ANSWERS?

A True Crime Story...

Tony Corley

Copyright © 2009 Tony Corley
The moral right of the author has been asserted.

Apart from any fair dealing for the purposes of research or private study, or criticism or review, as permitted under the Copyright, Designs and Patents Act 1988, this publication may only be reproduced, stored or transmitted, in any form or by any means, with the prior permission in writing of the publishers, or in the case of reprographic reproduction in accordance with the terms of licences issued by the Copyright Licensing Agency. Enquiries concerning reproduction outside those terms should be sent to the publishers.

ISBN: 9781848762534

A Cataloguing-in-Publication (CIP) catalogue record for this book is available from the British Library.

Typeset in 11pt Bembo by Troubador Publishing Ltd, Leicester, UK

Matador is an imprint of Troubador Publishing Ltd

ACKNOWLEDGEMENTS

Written in memory of Mark Corley.

First of all Id like to say a big thank you to the.. The Leicester mercury, the Melton times, and the Grantham journal newspapers for all their articles and advice. Secondly an organization called SAMM, Witch represents support after manslaughter and murder. Thirdly the person who helped me put this book together. I have told this story exactly in my own words and it is exactly how I feel, I have had to bring many bad memories flooding back to give the most honest story. I hope you appreciate I am not an author in any way I just hope this book will be of some interested to anybody, but especially to people who have gone through similar circumstances. Also to get my certain points over, for memory of my son Mark.

1

First of all I would like to say this book is written exactly how I tell my story.

The first time I heard the news about my son Mark Corley was in early June 2000. Mark was born in Leicester but moved to Grantham in Lincolnshire with his mother. I received a phone call from the town of Grantham, where the words of "dad" in a distressed voice on the phone were from my oldest daughter on the line. My first reaction was that there was obviously something wrong. She replied, "Mark has gone missing and we have been told something awful has happened to him." My reply was, "Don't be silly, what do you mean? He's okay it's just silly rumors."

More Questions than Answers?

After she then said, "We have been told Mark has possibly been, murdered." I just continued and said "Somebody's just having a joke, take no notice," but she insisted it was true, and had been told this information by somebody I didn't know. I told her "Not to worry, it's only words, he will turn up."

Little did I know... as the saying goes, you only think this sort of thing would happen to other people's families, – it's hard to imagine what it would feel like. Personally I never suspected anything, and just carried on as normal, until a few days later I received a phone call from Lincolnshire police asking if they could come to visit me. First I asked what it was about... if it was anything to do with Mark. After the conversation I had had with my daughter it was beginning to look like she had been right all along. All the panic was making sense; personally, I didn't want to believe that it was getting nearer to the truth. But the police wouldn't confirm anything over the phone until they visited me in person.

A few days after the phone call, two police officers paid a visit to my home in Leicester. They introduced themselves and I invited them in. They sat down and I made us all a drink. Everything was calm as they looked me up and down, now I know that they were obviously seeing how I was going to react to the news they were about to give me. Silence for a few seconds, then straight to the point. They told me the reason they had come was to do with my son, Mark Corley, who was 23 at the time. They said they had "information" that Mark has been lured away and murdered. Their enquiries up to that date, and acting on the information they already received – led them to believe that the news was almost certainly true.

I was told to "expect the worst."

My immediate reaction was blank; I refused to take it in. It's very strange, but I couldn't take it in as reality. I asked the police officers how they had got their information. And where was Mark? All I was told was they had lots of things they couldn't tell me, until they had done more of an investigation. They had suspects ready to bring in for questioning, but that was all I could be told for the time being. On leaving they left me a contact telephone number, and said they would keep me updated with any new information that came to light.

After the visit the strangest thing is that I didn't know what to think or to feel. I just didn't really believe any of it was true. I stayed as calm as I could, then after a while I made a call to my eldest daughter. She said, "It's best if you come over as we need to talk."

My wife also phoned me in a very upset state, almost hysterical. My words to her were, "Calm down and don't jump to conclusions – it's probably just still rumors." She told me that Mark's ex-girlfriend had explained to her that Mark was in danger, hanging around with the people he was with, and that they were planning to harm him, but that Mark was taking no notice. She also said that the police were almost certain that Mark had been murdered, and were bringing the suspects in for questioning. I asked who they were, but I wasn't familiar with any of them. The more questions I asked, the more sense I couldn't get… so I still didn't really believe any of it was true.

Thinking about the police and what had been said, I

More Questions than Answers?

knew they wouldn't just give that information for the fun of it. Deep down maybe I knew it was true, but I didn't want to believe it. It's like this... if the police had phoned me and said they wanted to visit me, had come in, sat down and said "We have news to give you... we've found your son's body – he's been murdered, and we can confirm it's him"... then that would have been a different approach to the whole situation. Perhaps I can say how I would have reacted to that kind of situation. It would have been more direct and hard hitting, instead of knowing that Mark was still out there and hadn't been found. Because at this stage, it was only talk to me – not reality. There was nothing factual. I'm not condemning the police, there was obviously truth in what I was being told.

Not long after the two police officers who had visited previously confirmed that the news was indeed true. They had also arrested several suspects. From then on, the same officers would be my police liaison, informing me of any news about Mark.

Now I was aware that he wouldn't be coming back, that the police were certain Mark wasn't going to be

More Questions than Answers?

coming back. The suspects were not co-operating, however; and it was just "No comment, no comment." I believe the police were acting as quickly as they could to get evidence, yet they could only tell me snippets of information for legal reasons, which I understood. Obviously, I had to wait for news, hoping that it would be good news. Colleagues would say "Keep your spirits up, you'll probably find he's just off visiting friends in another part of the country, and will show up."

As time started moving on I got no more information on what was happening. I had a phone call from a local Leicestershire newspaper, which had heard that Mark was missing and suspected murdered. They asked me for a photo and prepared an article. It was also printed in a Lincolnshire newspaper.

A day or two later I received a call from my liaison officers, explaining that they were trying to gather more evidence and they still had the five suspects in custody. They asked me if they could visit me in person again, instead of giving out information over the phone.

More Questions than Answers?

But I still couldn't take those visits seriously, because I still had hope that Mark was still out there – alive. But on this visit, both officers looked at me in a firm and straightforward manner and said, "Mark *has* been murdered – we are sorry to tell you. The people we have in custody may be charged with Mark's murder, but we have nothing at the moment to act on. Also, we have had numerous phone calls since the story went to press that Mark has been sighted in several parts of the country."

At the time I thought they must have doubted themselves, not sure whether Mark was alive, and that they had been acting on false information. One officer said that Mark had been seen in Bristol drinking in a bar. The local police were informed, and done an immediate check, but it turned out to be mistaken identity.

In that conversation again I was told to expect the worst. It was still strange because I couldn't fully take it in, but I think it was simply because I didn't want to believe it. Now, thinking back, I don't think the police were even sure themselves. They may have thought

More Questions than Answers?

they were being led on a wild goose chase. Before they left, the police again said I would be kept informed of any news, especially before anything went to the media (by law such news has to be told to the family of the victim first).

From that day on, time moved very slowly. All I could really do was hope that Mark was going to turn up. I visited Grantham and talked to my daughter, who was obviously very upset by rumors circulating in the town about what had happened to Mark. When I had spoke to Mark's mother, she was in a similar frame of mind as me – at the time we both thought there was still a possibility that Mark could still be alive.

She told me stories she had been told by other people, who'd said that Mark had been murdered by the five suspects the police had in custody. There was also a rumor that Mark had been killed and fed to pigs on a farm – all sorts of rumors, some far too sick to mention. Believe me, there are a lot of sick people out there. But also some very good people, though they are very hard to come by. It's very sad to say, especially when you hear news like that about your son.

More Questions than Answers?

As more weeks passed I had another phone call from Lincolnshire police. Again I was told that Mark was almost certainly dead, according to the new information they had gathered. I was told that Mark had been lured away by the five suspects police had in custody, and driven to an isolated area in Co. Durham, in the north east. Then he was shot in the back of the head. To me that was only something a callous coward could do.

The police also told me that one suspect had been charged with murder, and the other four had been charged with conspiracy to murder. All had been remanded at different prison locations around the country.

I still didn't believe it, I couldn't believe it was true. I asked why they had been heading to that part of the country, and why Mark had gone? They never did tell me. I heard rumors that two men were sent from Scotland to set Mark up to do a robbery, where a shotgun was involved. Allegedly, it turned out that these two men and three others from Grantham had been paid to lure Mark away and murder him. But if

More Questions than Answers?

this was the case, what could the motive possibly have been?

2

So there I was, sitting all alone trying to imagine what was going on, when my phone rings from the police liaison officers, who I put my trust in. To give me the service you would expect from the police, especially if it was to be in these circumstances. But some days would pass without any word whatsoever. It even got to the stage where I never bothered going to Grantham, because of all the pathetic, made up rumors and cheap talk. I just couldn't handle it.

Depression started kicking in – I just didn't know what to think or do, or who to turn to. Now, when I say I was on my own, I mean I was on my own. Truthfully, I didn't know where my friends were. It's

More Questions than Answers?

sad but it's true... so I had to start that tormented journey all on my own.

Don't get me wrong, I'm not looking for sympathy. Maybe this is one of the downfalls in my life, for not making enough friends, as some of the best friends I've had have, unfortunately, passed on or emigrated. From past experiences, these days I prefer my own company, but when something like this is sprung on you... I wished I could have had somebody to talk to. I didn't have anybody.

After my mother passed away in 1999, I and my closest family just seemed to drift apart. So as tough as it seems, I did just have to go with the flow, hoping the news I kept receiving was not true. I was still hoping that Mark was alive.

Lots of days I would just sit there and wait for my phone to ring, hoping to hear Mark on the other end. I was hoping to hear him say, "Dad, I am at wherever, could you come and pick me up?" Obviously, that was never going to be. But I still had my belief that Mark was still out there alive.

More Questions than Answers?

One day the phone call I got was not the phone call I wanted. It was Mark who I wanted on the other end of the phone, but instead it was my police liaison officers, asking me where I was and could they come and visit me with an update. I agreed, but on their arrival they started to talk about about the suspects they had charged with Mark's murder in detail. I interrupted and said, "How can you be certain? There is no proof and I think Mark is still alive."

They turned to me and said, "You're just going to have to accept that Mark is dead – it's just a matter of time before we find his body."

I looked at them and said, "Are you sure?" They stared straight at me and nodded firmly. "Yes."

I really didn't want to believe what they said was true. But it was my way of blocking out the truth. I was drained – mentally and physically.

So the police had got their suspects and had charged them with murder, but Mark was nowhere to be found. Oh God, what happens now? Mark's mum was in a terrible emotional state, so were my daughters. Even though we lived apart, it was not a pleasant thing to experience for any family.

So my anger was directed towards the suspects. Why had they done this? If it was true, which I still hoped it wasn't. When I'd asked the police, "What was the motive?" their story was, "We had several pieces of information some years back – when Mark was just a teenager he had supposedly thrown a stone, or an object of that description, at somebody's car whilst with a group of friends he palled around with." One friend who'd been a witness said that the person who owned the car had shouted at them, "I'm going to get you for this you mark my words." I wasn't told who the person was, but again there were rumors that the person had never forgotten the incident, and had held a grudge against Mark for it – and possibly for other things that I was never told about. Another rumor has it that this person plotted to have Mark lured away by the five suspects, and that he'd paid them to murder Mark.

That's the only motive I was ever told. It seems a big

More Questions than Answers?

price to pay for such a petty thing.

What kind of evil bastard could do this? This person obviously has more money than sense. What is this person, a so-called... gangster. If Mark was only a kid at the time and this thug has to carry a petty little incident for years as a grudge, then to pay somebody to take his life... I didn't think real so-called gangsters acted like kids themselves. Well what else can I say? I don't know, I'm in the dark.

Mark lived with me at certain times, and I tried to steer him in the right direction. At times he got himself into trouble. I'm not going to hide the fact that he was convicted for crimes such as shoplifting, and he had done the odd burglary, which I'm not proud of. Mark was punished and sent to young offenders' homes, and when he turned eighteen he moved on to a prison. The last time Mark was in prison I was hoping he would see sense. On his release we met up, and I truly believe he was beginning to mature, he seemed to have learnt his lesson. He actually told me he wanted to join the army. He wanted to get away from Grantham, and wanted no

More Questions than Answers?

more trouble. I told him, "Mark it's a shame you obviously don't know, but with a criminal record the army wouldn't entertain you." Mark wasn't aware of that at the time. And I wasn't aware that he was just going to go back into the same old company, petty crime and larking around. I really believe he could have moved on and made something of his life, because he was better than the so-called bad people, which is just what the media tried to label him as too.

I will never forget once when Mark was only sixteen I overheard a conversation where somebody was telling him lies. This person was convincing Mark that he could do more or less anything. If this bloke had told Mark he was God, I'm sure he would have believed him. After they had parted company I confronted Mark about those sorts of bullshitters, but Mark fell out with me. But I was only trying to get him to see some sense.

It was at that time that I realized Mark was very easily led. To then have been told that five people had asked him to go to Co. Durham to do a planned robbery sort of made sense. Mark would have believed this to

More Questions than Answers?

be true, and was obviously offered money to take part. We know now that it was just a trap to convince him. The shotgun that was to be used for the robbery was hidden in a field just outside Co. Durham. Little did Mark know that this was a plot for his murder, and no robbery.

The weeks passed and turned into months – five suspects still on remand for murder, and still no sign of Mark. I was getting more angry and frustrated because still the police couldn't tell me anything. I understood that for legal reasons they couldn't tell you everything, but I realize now that the police were only telling me what they wanted to tell me.

As time moved on I was beginning to sense more and more that the police were shifty, especially the more I asked them questions. It was more questions and more questions, but I never really got any answers – they couldn't answer. During some of the police investigations, they told me they had been back to some of the prisons where Mark had served time. The prison visits were to question some of the longer serving inmates. Having some of the inmates been

More Questions than Answers?

questioned the police told me, "Mark had done some wrong doing whilst inside." I said I didn't understand. What was the worst thing you could do in prison? Steal somebody's tobacco or chocolate? Would that be enough to have somebody murdered? I still don't understand...

However, I have heard rumors; people have said that Mark's murder was to do with drug dealing, saying that's the only reason people get shot these days, which clearly isn't the case. Everybody seems to jump to that conclusion. The police never mentioned to me anything related to drugs, in fact they never gave me any motive other than the one I mentioned earlier, about the so-called gangster. Other than that, I asked many other questions but never really got any answers. So what was I to believe? Sick and traumatized with worry, sleepless nights, and also the number of people who have said, "I'm sorry, I can understand what you're going through."

There was a time when I turned to somebody and said, "Do you understand? Are you in the same predicament as me right now?" They couldn't answer

More Questions than Answers?

me. That's why I would prefer some people to just think and put their brain into gear. Some people just can't help themselves – how can they understand if they are not going through the same situation or, same circumstances? Perhaps they are just trying to help. I would sooner people just say they are sorry, instead of telling me they understand.

I can tell you this much. Let's say that if it was drugs Mark was dealing in, first, I have never known him to have large amounts of money to flash round, nor flash cars, fancy holidays or jewellry. Second, he had never mentioned to me that he had ever done drugs (only the odd bit of cannabis, which seems normal these days – what teenager doesn't experiment in that way?).

I do know certain company Mark socialized with used harder drugs. Yet I would have known if he had anything to do with dealing drugs, and I'm almost certain he didn't. Another thing is, what could have been the motive? People said his murder was to do with drugs, and he may have dealt with somebody in the drugs world – he may have owed money. This may have led whoever it was to get revenge, but again, I

More Questions than Answers?

was never told by any of the police officers that drugs were involved in any way at all.

Time was moving on and still no sign of Mark's whereabouts. If he was dead or alive. There was plenty of media that believed Mark had been murdered, but I still wanted to believe that he was still out there, alive. The time was now September 2000, four months after the first news I received about Mark being missing. The whole situation was a total nightmare – what could I do? I had no choice, I just had to carry on the best I could, still wanting to hear Mark's voice on the other end of the phone. I was just waiting. If I went into Grantham, all I would hear was sick, pathetic rumors. It disgusted me. I went into my own corner, so to speak, and waited for news from my liaison officers, expecting it to be honest and upfront. How wrong I was. More often than not, something about the police officers always made me feel suspicious. I put it down to stress and the situation I was in, but long after I still felt the same way. I'm disgusted the way I was treated.

I suppose it's like people who discussed the situation with me have said – a small police force in a small

More Questions than Answers?

town like Grantham are never prepared for situations like that. They just couldn't handle it; they aren't like the Metropolitan police, which is fully prepared, and which would have handled the situation a lot better. Unfortunately, I just got dealt with by inexperienced police officers. Most people who I talk to now, people who have gone through similar situations to me, who have lost a son or a daughter, have all agreed that I was unlucky to get poor liaison officers. These people were so pleased that they had had good liaison officers... but that wasn't the case with me.

Now we were into December 2000, Christmas approaching, not something I was looking forward to. I was walking around in a trance, the lights, music, everything – it didn't mean anything. Only the thought of Mark out there... as I must admit, now I was beginning to think it was true, he was out there somewhere, having been murdered by those cowards. Evil bastards, to take somebody and kill them in cold blood – shot in the back of the head – to me that's not a man, that's not even human, it's a total coward. It was the 13th of December and I received a phone call from a family member saying they had heard the news on television that the remains of a body had been found on the outskirts of Durham. And that it was certain to be the body of Mark Corley of Grantham. So that was it. The news I didn't want to hear… finally it was true. It was all on the news. I was panicking, and my wife wasn't really talking to me due to all the upset. I didn't have anyone to turn to; I thought, why haven't my liaison officers been in touch?

Eventually, two or three hours after Mark's body had been found and the news was all over the press, the officers telephoned me. I said I had already heard, and asked why I had to hear it from someone else. They were dealing with another situation, they said, and apologized. "It doesn't matter now, my son's dead anyway," I said. They didn't really seem that much bothered.

I was asked if I was all right, and if there was anybody here with me. I just said, "What's the point?" I hung up the phone, and have never had any more contact. From then on I relied on information from the media. Personally, I think it's disgraceful, the way I was treated

More Questions than Answers?

by my liaison officers. They never came to me as if they were interested; I suppose because I and my wife had been separated it was more convenient for the police to inform her of any details, as well as Mark's ex girlfriend... and her parents too! But not his father.

I could never understand why I was last on their list. I had to rely on phones calls for news from a friend or family, I was constantly fobbed off. Walking home one day from the local town, I noticed a car parked outside my house. The people in the car turned out to be two plain clothed police officers, neither of whom were my liaison officers. As I got to my front door they both stepped out the car and approached. They asked my name, which I confirmed, and I said "Have you come here about Mark?" They said, "No, we're from Lincolnshire police and we're here to search your premises." I replied, "For what reason?" They said, "We have reason to believe you are in possession of a firearm."

I was very annoyed to say the least, but knowing that you have to take it seriously, knowing that someone had made such an allegation.. I told them to take their time and feel free until they were fully satisfied, as I had nothing to hide. Having done their search, they said they didn't think for one moment that I was in possession of a firearm. My reply was, "Well can you answer me one question? Why have you come all this way to search me when you didn't believe I had a weapon in the first place?" Their reply was, "We have been sent by our boss to do a routine search." Can you imagine? I was so upset, my son had been found dead, five suspects were remanded in custody charged with his murder, and I get dealt with in that way. And some devious bastard is wasting police time, with false information about me having a gun. I told the police that the nearest to a real gun I had owned was a plastic toy gun I had as a young child... plus a cowboy outfit!

So now reality had kicked in, and my wife was blaming me. I'd be a liar if I said I wasn't blaming her too. It was just ill-feeling all round, turning very nasty... and my youngest daughter wouldn't speak to me. I had to rely on my eldest daughter to give me any information about Mark's funeral arrangements and so on. Again I couldn't understand why the police liaison officers were not in contact with me about any

More Questions than Answers?

of this. I felt like a total stranger, I felt more like Mark's stepfather than his real father. Surely there was some explanation for all, this but I never received one. The more I asked questions, the fewer answers I got. It was just make your own mind up, go with your instinct. Can you imagine – I was stood at my wife's door three days before Christmas, apologizing for what had happened. She just said, "Go away, please just go away", then broke down in tears and closed the door. I respected what she wanted, which was to be left alone, realizing this woman I had married had brought Mark into the world. That's what was going through my mind as I drove home with tears streaming down my face – three days before Christmas and realizing how life can be so cruel. One year ago to the day I was sitting having a laugh and a joke, a cup of tea with her, and even though we were separated, we kept in touch and got on quite well. Then it all changed after Mark's death. I suppose somebody has to blame somebody.

Thinking back, Mark was old enough to know right from wrong,. He was a clean living lad who always kept himself smart for those who knew him. He had a sense of humor; I never will really get straight

More Questions than Answers?

answers to what happened, I have not tried to hide anything. Mark did get into trouble and was punished for it, I tried to put him on the right track and give the right advice, but as a parent you can only do so much. I do know he wasn't an out and out heroin addict. All I can think is that it was something really pathetic for somebody to have murdered him. Maybe it was something very big with lots of money involved, or something Mark knew that was in the underground gang world, and was so secret that it obviously cost him his life. As I said, Mark was easily led, somebody out there wanted him dead and they got what they wanted.

I haven't got what I wanted... an explanation. Why was he murdered? If it's true that Mark's ex-partner pleaded with him not to go on the journey with those five people, who turned out to be the five suspects. Apparently she knew something, told him he was going to be harmed by them, and that he was in danger. But I was told he never took it seriously, truthfully I find it all very strange. If it was all just about a damaged car and somebody had thrown a stone at it, then yes, I would agree it's enough to make

More Questions than Answers?

anybody angry if it was dealt with there and then with a firm clip around the ear. But to plot some years after to have Mark lured away and killed... I find that very hard to understand, especially if that is the only motive. In fact, if as I have been told, the motive was more to do with drugs, even though I'm not certain, and no police officer involved in the case has confirmed this to me, I'm still not sure – it's all confusing, I know. So another question, again, is still what was the motive?

I suppose it doesn't matter to the public out there which reads newspapers, because the media always prints what they believe themselves most of the time. The things the media said about Mark at the time were not nice, especially when it's your own son in the spotlight. The media have a way with words, so someone who never knew Mark will draw assumptions, because of the circumstances of the murder, and as he was from a basic working class background they just label him as scum. It's just sad for people who judge a person on what the media print.

I have met young lads and thought to myself, they

look like trouble, yet how wrong I have been. When they've approached me to ask the time or for directions, I found them very polite. People always jump to conclusions about people's appearance these days – "you can't judge a book by its cover." There is a true story I heard in London, that a young couple were searching for an apartment to rent. When they went for the interview, the estate agent turned them down. The female partner said, "What was the problem?" After a few days, to check to see if they had been accepted, they found the estate agent was pointing out the couples' dress standard – bearing in mind the young couple were both in full time employment and respectable! The girl replied to the estate agent, saying, "I suppose you would prefer it if we both wore suits and ties?" to which his reply was, "It would be a good idea, yes." Her instant reply was, "No thank you, we would rather not, as the Kray twins used to wear suits." I rest my case.

3

At that point Christmas was gone, it was a new year but everything was still so confusing. Now I was waiting for the trial, but still not knowing when Mark's body was going to be released for a funeral. Again I wasn't told anything by the police. Instead I was told by a family member that we couldn't have a body release date due to a post-mortem and forensic examination. I just told myself, "When my son is laid to rest, then the trial begins," which really was keeping me sane and holding me together. I just wanted to see the people who had conspired to murder my son be punished, hoping they would go to prison for a long time. It was a long wait, but I was told again by a family member, not the police liaison, that a trial date

More Questions than Answers?

for the accused was to be fixed at Nottingham Crown Court for late January or February 2002. The next I heard was from my eldest daughter, as my wife was now totally ignoring me. The news was about Mark's body, and that a funeral date was being fixed. Surprisingly enough, on this occasion the police did contact me with this small detail, which I was surprised by.

Mark's funeral took place in April 2001 at Grantham Crematorium. I was told the police were satisfied with all the forensics, and so on, and that they had enough evidence. The police told me to "trust them", and that the suspects were "going to go to prison for a long time – but in the meantime, let's give Mark a good send off and pay our respects."

When I got to the Catholic Church in Grantham for the burial service, I couldn't understand why I was asked by two plain clothed police officers at the door of the church to identify myself. Having told them who I was, they eventually agreed to let me in. I never really did ask about this because I would never have got any proper answers. After the service, Mark's last

More Questions than Answers?

journey was to the cemetery, where he was laid to rest. God bless him. Funerals are not my best subject. I don't suppose anybody in their right mind likes them, but one way or another, it's a fact of life we have to face up to.

Something else that has always made me think, why? When I was looking at the flowers and wreaths at the funeral at the time, when colleagues, friends and family were making their way to the wake, I began to notice one of the liaison police officers hanging around the grave. I still never got to know why the police were hanging around the service and burial, because when I asked questions I never got any answers.

Even at the wake there were police officers. I never really socialized with anybody that day, I preferred to be alone. In fact, in my opinion, most of the people there were taking the piss. When you think of the circumstances of all this, the family deserved some peace and respect, yet all I felt was unease. Maybe the police were there, expecting trouble. I was told by one person that they were expecting the murder suspect's family to gatecrash, and cause trouble at the funeral. It

More Questions than Answers?

also has been stated, and had gone to press, that one police officer had received a death threat by text message from one of the suspect's girlfriends – who was later charged with threatening a police officer. When the case went to court she was acquitted, and the case thrown out. Apparently, according to her, it was meant as a joke. I'm sure all the evidence was there. If it was sent by text, my question again is, why?

So now Mark was laid to rest – no parent can really explain how it feels, unless they have gone through this kind of experience. I always say you would be surprised by the rudeness of some people in this world – even today people know the situation about my son. You would think I'd get some peace, but people have often said, "Are you not over it yet?" I don't know whether to feel sorry for them, or to shout and scream at them. But no, I realize now after so many years that you have to learn to understand that if they have not been through the same circumstances, or anything similar, they don't understand. Let's face it, all murders are different, but none are pleasant to any family, no matter what circumstances. I know I will never get over this, it's true that you learn to live with

More Questions than Answers?

it, but believe me, it's very hard. It turns your life upside down, you feel as though you are just labelled and that you are different, that people have an attitude towards you. Most people I know from meetings who have lost a family member through murder say exactly the same thing. Yet really we shouldn't be feeling this way, we have done nothing wrong, this sort of thing can happen to anybody in the world. I wished it had never happened to me and my family, but it did, and there is nothing I can do to turn the clock back.

It's really traumatizing, panic attacks and nightmares,, which way do I turn? All the stories I heard from this person, from that person... who do you believe? Who do you trust? Why didn't the police keep me informed, up to date and on time before the news went to press? There is no excuse really.

Little did I know, it was going to get even worse. Don't take me the wrong way; I have every respect for the police and what they have to deal with on a day to day basis, terrible tragedies all over the world. Where would we be without them? I have met some very nice police officers on my travels, and have also met some very unsociable ones. There is good and bad in all professions. So I am not having any direct criticism towards the police in general, I'm just making my point about the police who dealt with Mark's murder case. To me it was very unprofessional from start to finish. I'm very disappointed by the way I was treated by my liaison officers. If their approach had been different it would have helped to cushion the blow.

Now I believe that the officers who dealt with Mark's case were not trained for this kind of situation. I am so angry, frustrated, Mark's disappearance was upsetting enough, but then to be missing for six months, it was mental torture throughout. Then to be told he had been found murdered... add all this up together, try and push it out of your mind, forget it, and move on – could anybody say that's possible? I don't think so. It's destroyed me, it has broken up my family nine years on, and I'm still trying to pick the pieces up and move on with my life. I find it very difficult, believe me.

Most days when I turn the television on, the news tells you of a murder – somebody's son, daughter or

More Questions than Answers?

whoever it could be, killed by knife or gun crime, or whatever. It's not pleasant, and it reminds me of my circumstances and what we have been through. I wish the law would change in this country and really clamp down, dish out harder punishment and make criminals think twice about committing such callous crimes.

It's so frightening and depressing. How can I put the loss of Mark behind me and block it out, when I pick a newspaper or watch TV and there is news of a similar event every day – believe me it's hard.

4

Now it was coming to the end of January 2002 and the trial was being prepared at Nottingham Crown Court. The accused were driven to court each day to sit in front of the judge while he read the paperwork to prepare for the trial. I was told certain news by my daughter, who phoned and asked if I wanted to take a trip to Nottingham. I am still none the wiser why we went that day, to be honest, bearing in mind the case hadn't even fully started yet. It was just all paperwork and legal argument. The five accused were sitting facing the judge as we peered through the doors we could see into the court room. We couldn't hear any conversation, and obviously I'm not good at lip reading. My eldest daughter discreetly nodded to me,

More Questions than Answers?

in a way pointing out which one had been charged as the main murder suspect. And the other four who had conspired.

After about five minutes the suspects actually noticed us peering through the door and made snide comments to each other – one actually looked straight towards us. I don't know if they knew me as Mark's father as they have never seen me before, nor had I seen them. They mean nothing to me. They possibly knew my daughters, but what did shock me and hurt me on the day was the fact that two of them were sniggering between each other, the fact that we were standing looking at them, they obviously knew who we were, but they showed no emotion. I had to leave and just hoped the trial would start early that next week. I couldn't stand their attitude, knowing they were the suspects in Mark's murder. After all, you're talking about a human being, and to them it was all like it was all a joke.

I decided to go home and try and chill out, but a few days after I had a phone call from my eldest daughter saying my wife wanted to talk to me and could I come

More Questions than Answers?

over. I arranged to go over to Grantham one evening, and on my arrival, when I met my daughter, she said, "Would you like to go and see your granddaughter?" as that's where my wife was with Mark's ex-partner. When we got there I could sense an atmosphere. Everybody was edgy; my wife apparently had just left. I asked if everything was okay. Mark's ex-partner's parents were there with my granddaughter; they looked at me and said, "No." Automatically I said, "What do you mean?" They said that they had just had a phone call from Nottingham Crown Court, from the police liaison officers and the inspector in charge of the case. They had said that "Things are not looking good." I couldn't believe what I was hearing, and said "No wonder my wife has left in such an angry mood." But they said not to jump to conclusions.

During this time, Mark's ex-partner had a phone call from one of the officers who told us to stay put as they needed to have a word. On their arrival, after a couple of hours, they calmly walked in. As far as I was concerned, they might as well have just got straight to the point, but I don't think they did. It was about the wrongful doing they had done. They had illegally

More Questions than Answers?

planted secret recording devices to listen in on the suspects, they'd bugged the police exercise yards. The judge had said, "The trial cannot go ahead because of a breach in the human right's act, and the suspects were entitled to certain privacy. The law itself was broken by the police, planting bugging devices in the exercise yards, and listening in on the suspects' conversations with solicitors." According to form, the police bugged the exercise yards on two other cases they were investigating, which I was not aware of until long after. I turned to the police officers and said, "So that's it? They are going to walk free tomorrow.?" They could only say, "It's looking that way now, yes."

All the waiting to get justice, I just didn't know what to think, were they joking? Surely not. I just walked to the door in anger. I remember the boss in charge of the case was always fairly reasonable throughout; as strange as it may seem, I did somehow sympathize with him because he showed some concern in his mistake for the police's wrong-doing, and I would say he was coming up to retirement around that time anyway. As for the other officer who was classed as one of my liaison officers, well he just stared at me. He couldn't understand why I was so angry. Maybe it was his nerves, but I noticed he sort of grinned. I thought 'You're just taking piss' – that particular officer never showed any emotion. That was it for me, and I walked out and went straight home, no phone call from any officers the next day.

The next evening I turned the television on to see that five suspects had been told they were free to go from Nottingham Crown Court after several months on remand after being charged with the murder of Mark Corley. It was all too much to take in. The Lincolnshire police had let me and my family down. They broke the law themselves, and let five suspects get away with murder. The police had told me that they had enough evidence to send these suspects away for a long time – and yet now they can't understand why I'm angry with them! Why did they do it? Why couldn't they have just done their jobs correctly and legally? Then the suspects would have had a fair trial and justice would have been done. The police didn't make a mistake; they knew they were breaking the law.

This experience will stay with me for the rest of my

More Questions than Answers?

life. Those people walked free under the human right's act, yet I was treated like I was doing wrong. I sometimes wonder if the police wanted some information to bug the exercise yards that way, and it was also pointed out by the judge, they broke the law by doing this. Could it have been done deliberately... who knows? Maybe the police wanted the case to be dropped for some reason? Bearing in mind that trials cost millions of pounds — but Mark was a human being. Let's also bear in mind that Mark came from a working class family, and I hear that the police never liked him. I believe that if the police had wanted the trial to go ahead, it would have done. But it didn't. Was it because it was Lincolnshire police again?

5

So there I was, thinking to myself what happens next? Surely the police are going to be punished for their wrongful doing, they broke the law? Well one thing was for sure, I couldn't concentrate my anger after all this, which way do I turn? What do I do now? Sit and wait in silence? Of course it was all in the media headlines; it also made the front pages of two national newspapers to my knowledge. That night I was lying in bed listening to a debate on a radio station where the subject came up about the collapse of the trial. They were actually reading the newspapers for the forthcoming day as it was the early hours of the morning, and it was stated that the court trail was the first ever to collapse under the human right's act. I was

More Questions than Answers?

> ### Officers suspended for 'bugging abuse'
> **By Jacqui Walls**
> Thursday, 31 January 2002   SHARE   PRINT ARTICLE   EMAIL ARTICLE   A A TEXT SIZE
>
> Three detectives were suspended from operational duties yesterday over accusations by a judge that police had illegally bugged five men accused of a murder plot.
>
> An investigation is being held by Lincolnshire police after the trial of the five men accused of conspiring to kill Mark Corley was thrown out at Nottingham Crown Court.
>
> Detective Chief Inspector Tony White, Detective Inspector Roger Bannister and Detective Sergeant Steve Thorn have been taken off all operational duties pending a Police Complaints Authority inquiry.
>
> A spokesman for Lincolnshire police said: "We fully recognise the serious nature of the comments made by Mr Justice Newman at Nottingham Crown Court and understand the media and public concern arising out of this case ... Lincolnshire police have taken three detective officers off all operational duties."
>
> Mr Corley's mother, Eileen, vowed to continue her fight for justice. She was "absolutely devastated" that no one had been convicted over the death of her son, whose body was found in a field in Co Durham in December 2000, five months after he was shot in the head.
>
> Nottingham Crown Court was told that hidden microphones had been installed at two police stations, recording conversations between the accused and their solicitors.
>
> Robert Sutherland, 36, of Bathgate, West Lothian, pleaded not guilty to murder. He also denied conspiracy to murder with John Smith, 27, Gary Self, 36, Danny Gray, 21, and John Toseland, 59, from Grantham.

© Independent Newspapers Ltd

so disappointed when they commented on Mark; it's the way they put it across and said he was known to be a villain, they were criticizing him, but they obviously didn't know the full story. Typical media, they were talking as if Mark deserved what happened to him. For them it's always okay for them to give any old cock and bull story so they can fill their air time up with garbage to make a story. Half of the time they don't know what they are fucking talking about. As long as it's not themselves they are criticizing they are okay, but when it's your son who has been murdered it's hard to take in all the rubbish they talk. Also they

More Questions than Answers?

mentioned a possibility of what could have happened to the police officers. Sadly enough they were not charged for breaking the law – they should have been in my opinion. They were only disciplined – yes only disciplined – for breaking the law which led to five suspects of murder walking free and carrying on with life. I never had one personal visit from those police officers, never one apology. Even to this day it's taken me years to learn to live with the way I was treated by them, and I'll never get over it. I'll always think there was a mystery over the whole case, in my opinion; others are entitled to theirs too.

After all of that I just lost the plot, drinking alcohol, but the problem is still there the next day. Why couldn't they have done their job right? They say nobody is above the law, but every now and again I often think to myself, those five suspects who murdered Mark were above the law, especially when I saw their attitude on the news when the press approached them as they walked free. The arrogance, they are not men, just cowards. I think the police were never bothered either way, I always believe they had it in for Mark, which is still wrong. I don't think it was

More Questions than Answers?

ever meant to be for a fair trial or any kind of justice. I know myself from my experience with those liaison officers, from their body language, something was never right. Maybe some people think, what is my point? There could be several points. Especially when you are left in the dark like I was throughout the whole case. The fact that I never lived in Grantham and the fact that the police had to travel that extra journey was no excuse; the technology we have nowadays could have been used, but they couldn't even be bothered to phone me.

So let's just get all this straight; my son goes missing for six months then is eventually found murdered, the five suspects charged of his murder walk free, all because the police can't do their job right, and deliberately broke the law. So what am I supposed to do? Walk around with a smile on my face as if nothing has happened. I'm sorry I can't do that, it would never be possible, but that's what the police expected me to do, push all the misery under the carpet. Excuse me, you're talking about a human being here, my son. Well I take it they have all moved on with their lives now. I suppose one day the real truth will come out, if God prevails. I think some people have no conscience, they can go to bed and sleep, but I can't. I have fucking nightmares and horrible panic attacks.

As things settled down after the trial, there was one last hope, and that was for the police to be punished for their wrong-doing. That dragged on for some time but as you know they were not charged, only lightly disciplined. The top boss who was due for retirement anyway was just demoted to a lower ranking. Again I hear rumors that one officer emigrated to Australia after suffering a nervous breakdown, I wonder why? Others were transferred here and there, it's all history now.

I wish I could move on like them and put the past behind me. It's only years after that I have been pointed to an organization called victim support. I was told by a friend about it – I can never understand why they didn't approach me from word go, which was the normal thing to do – another point I have to make, about the police who never helped me in that way. Every solicitor I went to to try and take some action against the police for their wrong-doing just kept

More Questions than Answers?

going round in circles. All they said was that they sympathized, but I was wasting my time. Six months after the trial had collapsed there was a new Chief Inspector in charge at Grantham police station – he was familiar with the trial and was looking in to see if anything else could be done.

I phoned him and made an appointment to go along and see him. Of course I wanted to express my feelings and say how I felt about the way I was treated, but it was in an abrupt manner. On my arrival at Grantham police station I met the new chief inspector and he invited me into his office. I explained my feelings and how I had been treated. He took a statement and said he would look into it and talk to the officers. Also he would contact me by telephone or he would write to me to let me know the outcome. Four months after that I still had no reply. I still had no news that the officers had been punished, but they never were. As much as I tried in my own way to get on from day to day, an uphill struggle that that still is, one day I just decided that he was never going to let me know anything about my complaint, so I decided to give him a call. I had waited long enough and I was very patient, considering all the shit I had gone through. When I finally got through, he just came over in the calmest of manners – it seemed as if he was not familiar with the case, not even slightly bothered. That is how he put it over the phone. What could I do? Weak, powerless, drained. Emotionally broken I really had no more to say, I couldn't. My family and I had lost, what more could I do?

What I did do was turn to alcohol, which is an honest answer. I still know to this day that it has never solved any of my problems. A relationship I was in at the time was broken, family drifted apart so now I'm on my own, left with broken pieces to pick up. You can't mend this kind of situation; you can't even explain to someone who has not been through the same experience because they just don't understand. Even now, nine years on, I still can't cope, I'm a completely different person.

I can't get over it. I have tried – if I could find a way to get over these sorts of tragedies I would be out there helping other people.

6

Two years later I had moved to a new area thinking and hoping that I could move on. But no such thing, nobody to turn to really. I am still trapped in my own world of depression. Three years further down the line my father passed on – he hadn't been very well since my mother passed away in 1999, and he suffered with Alzheimer's disease. I feel sad about this because he was never really aware of what was happening – it's very upsetting to see somebody going through that. Two of the best people in the world, your mother and father, who are your best friends. Even to this day I miss them so much. When people say, "You will miss them when they have gone", never has a truer word been spoken. I will always have the greatest respect for them. I am proud to be their son, knowing they were liked by many people.

I was travelling to a meeting recently when I boarded the bus to sit down. A nice old gentleman got on and sat down next to me. We just struck up a little conversation about the weather and things, the usual really. We both agreed on the same things such as doom and gloom being hyped up, things like the recession and the weather; we had both obviously seen colder winters. When it came to his stop for getting off the bus I wished him all the best and thanked him for our little conversation. He turned and said, "No problem at all it didn't cost us anything did it?" Then in his next breath he said, "That's where the world has gone wrong these days." I thought, he is right there – there's a lack of communication. He was an old Irish gentleman, the same country my father came from. When he left the bus it just brought memories back to me about when I used to sit and talk to my father, little moments like that mean a lot to me, moments of happiness. I know a lot of people criticize the older generation, but there are many pleasant people out there. I love to meet them and could talk for hours on

More Questions than Answers?

end at every opportunity. It takes all kinds, young or old.

I was still trying to learn to live with my trauma, even though it's easier said than done. Eventually, I had a phone call from a counselling service which knew I was walking around in circles banging my head against the wall, in a sense. The reality of it all was, what was the point of me talking to people who didn't understand? So after nine years the counselling service came up with information about an organization called SAMM – Support After Manslaughter and Murder. The person I spoke to from the counselling service mailed me the address and telephone numbers of SAMM's head office in Birmingham. I did wonder why it had taken nine years for me to receive such information, especially in this day and age. Even victim support was not suggested to me by my police liaison officers during the early stages of the murder case. I have heard people get a letter from victim support, offering support over incidents such as petty things like a gang of teenagers loitering around a person's property maybe meaning no harm, but it's intimidating. People get victim support for those kinds of situations, but I was never offered anything like that and my son was murdered.

I was ready to try anything to ease the pain of what I have been through. So I decided to make the phone call. The lady I spoke to asked me my details and explained about the organization. She said they ran meetings around most parts of England, and the nearest location to me was in Sheffield in Yorkshire. She told me a lot of people go along to the meetings and decide it's not for them, and also that the meetings were hard to keep together as people found it hard to drag memories and feelings back during discussion. I was told I was more than welcome to attend the meeting in Sheffield, held each month. I decided to attend – I thought, what do I have to lose? In fact hopefully I could benefit.

I arranged to get to Sheffield, knowing it was only a two hour meeting and a fair journey ahead and back. I was very nervous, but ten minutes after my arrival and introduction I was fine. Coffee and biscuits were available, and then we sat round. Each person introduced themselves and only if they wanted could

More Questions than Answers?

explain their tragic loss and circumstances – most bravely did, including me. For once it made me feel I was not alone, all those other people around me had gone through many similar circumstances.

I attended this meeting on my own through my own choice. Even though it was only two hours it soon passed very quickly. Coming away from that meeting I was amazed at some of the different circumstances, but I can honestly say from time to time, as I will explain further on, that the odd person has said to me, "Oh God, I don't know how you have coped with getting no trial or victim support after all these years."

So I decided to pay a few more visits and got to know a few of the other members, who I still keep in contact with. But after a while, I thought that every month was a bit too much travelling to Sheffield, and I didn't want to keep dragging the same subjects up each time, so I backed off a little at times. After one more meeting I decided to call it quits and said my farewells.

Some time after that I had a phone call from the SAMM head office, which was formerly based in

More Questions than Answers?

London. I said it was a pity there were no meetings closer to where I lived, and they said that if ever there happened to be one up and running I would be contacted. I was asked if I had ever been on a training day. I was unfamiliar and asked what it meant; I was told the next time a training day became available I should travel to London or Birmingham, and spend the night in a hotel. I did this, and most of the day was spent in a conference room discussing all kinds of situations of homicide, how to deal with stress and anger, all different kinds of situations. Also, you could volunteer to set up your own meetings in your area, or do phone voluntary work for other victims in similar situations. This could be somebody who has lost a family member through murder.

I found the whole thing very helpful and interesting. The people all related together, even though again the situation was different, we could all benefit and comfort each other. SAMM have been very helpful, they have even organized and invited me to a retreat in a very quiet and peaceful location. All the members who attended that meeting with me had lost sons and daughters, some had lost sisters, car accidents, murders

More Questions than Answers?

some crimes had been solved, others not but, we all related in some way. I have made friends with these members and am still keeping in contact, and I hope to for years to come. It is these people who are keeping me going at the moment. I would recommend SAMM to anybody in these situations. It was well worth the wait. I really do appreciate what they have done for me and they are always there if I need them – they deserve every donation, and anybody can donate. In fact I could never really express my true feelings in words; SAMM to me has helped more than any psychiatrist, psychologist or counsellor put together. I do hope more people get to hear about SAMM. It amazes me the people that go through circumstances like me, although all are different to mine. Some of the members I have come across have a lot of built up anger which I fully understand – it's only natural, let's face it. After all is said and done, you can't just brush things under the carpet.

I have said before there are a lot of people who think it's as easy as that, but like I'm saying again it's not so easy. You would be surprised at the number of people

More Questions than Answers?

who have never experienced these traumas who say to me, "Go for revenge". Well, that's easier said than done — and I wouldn't consider it anyway. You would also be surprised that people in the same situation as me, over the years, have lost loved ones through murder; I have never read about or known of anybody who has taken revenge. Then I get people who say, "What goes around comes around, and the offenders will get their payback — and revenge will come to them in different way." I am not a big believer in that. I was brought up as a Catholic, my parents came from southern Ireland, where most of the population is Catholic. I don't go to church every Sunday, but I do believe there is a God. We all know there are too many arguments about religion in this world. Personally, I respect everybody's religion; everybody is entitled to believe in what they want.

Some time back I must admit I broke the rules of my religion, I went to a spiritualist medium, which the Catholic religion is against. But only because I had read some books and watched certain programs on TV where several people claimed they had contacted the dead. So there is another side so we are told by

More Questions than Answers?

these people – when we pass on we still have our spirit around our family. I have never seen a ghost, but I have spoken to people over the years who claim they have. Most stories I think are total bullshit, but I must admit that certain people have told me stories that I have no reason to doubt. In fact I really think I believe them. There have been certain occasions since Mark passed away, such as pictures falling from walls, lights failing, things too obvious not to be a coincidence. The more I think about these occurrences, the more I am convinced that something is out there. Even though I am still skeptical, I keep an open mind. I would never condemn any of it – I would only tell the truth about the experiences I have had. I wouldn't just say things like, "I've seen a ghost" for the sake of it. I do still believe in God, and I believe there is something out there.

One of my strongest beliefs is fate, things happen for a reason. Lots of people I talk to say it's coincidence, then when you discuss spirits, life after death, etc., lots of people believe it. Then again, lots of people says it's total rubbish – "When you're gone, your gone". Lots of people make a good living out of spiritualism. I

More Questions than Answers?

don't think I'll be going to see those kind of people anymore as, truthfully, you're only looking for contact with the dead. If the dead are meant to get in touch with us then they will – or maybe it happens in other ways, like strange mysterious things happening that are unexplainable. That's why I just like to leave things the way they are now. For lots of people it can bring them comfort, but there is everything out there that still remains to be seen and proven 100%. I have heard stories from people, who couldn't have had better proof from a sprit medium, and they have still told me they will remain skeptical – it's their way of not wanting to believe it's true.

A friend of mine who I met at the SAMM meetings sat opposite me one evening when the subject was brought up about life after death. I asked him if he was a believer; he shook his head and said, "No my belief is, when you're gone you're gone. There are a lot of clever people out there who make money from that sort of thing, – if somebody was to prove and convince me otherwise I would be open-minded, but nobody ever has." The sad story was that his daughter was followed back to school, having gone home for lunch

More Questions than Answers?

that day, by a lone stalker in a van who abducted her. The stalker took her to a disused quarry where she was raped and murdered, a terrible ordeal. I'm unsure back in the seventies whether the victim's family had liaison officers, but the gentleman told me that when the suspect was caught and charged a police officer told him the date of the court appearances. Especially when it came up to the main sentence, he and his family were told, "You remain calm in the court, no talking or shouting whatsoever". The convicted person was sentenced to prison in Broadmoor indefinitely, and still is there to this day, as I'm told. The victim's family left the court and has never had any more contact with the police, so basically all they were given were dates of court appearances and told not to obstruct the trial in any way. In other words, there were no liaison officers as such. This gentleman doesn't know himself if police liaison officers even existed – was that the normal system in those days? It certainly seems to me, even though this gentleman got justice, I perhaps would have been better off being cut out short and given certain dates instead of being fobbed off about things by my so-called police liaison officers. At least I would have known where I stood from word go, like this gentleman knew where he stood.

Yet other members of SAMM had a great relationship with the police. All my police officers did was make me feel like I was the offender. I'm still very upset — perhaps if I was a doctor or a schoolteacher I would have been treated better, I don't know. Was it personal? I still don't know. I don't know why the police never came to my door after all the disaster, when everything had gone wrong, and apologized, even though it wouldn't have made any difference. I would still feel slightly better if they had apologized. Maybe it would have given me just some confidence in them.

Right up to last moment local news reporters were visiting my wife's house in Grantham to do an evening news report. This is really the last time I ever spoke to her, because there were too many people hanging around. Their attitude towards me again was stale — I always got the feeling they never wanted me there. I made it clear how I felt. I told my wife, "They are just making more of a fool of you now, don't you understand? Tell them to leave, all the damage has been done its now like a circus." She was obviously too

More Questions than Answers?

upset to understand anything that was happening, again she didn't know who her true friends were; to me they are just a load of scandalmongers. It's sad that we couldn't have got together and discussed it in a calmer manner. I would have been there throughout – it's a shame we couldn't. I always did my best for Mark, I was there when he needed me; he knew that and so did she. I always wanted what was best for him, not to be hanging around with scum. People may laugh, but there was more of a good side to Mark, deep down than anybody will know. If he was tougher and up front and not so vulnerable and easily lead, he would still be here today. I was never fully aware of what was going on, I never delved into his business. Even though he had got into situations where he was sent to prison, on his release I just hoped for him eventually to see the light and grow up. I really did hope he would move on for the better, but obviously that wasn't meant to be. Since that visit to my wife's that day, I have never spoken to or seen her. Maybe she is still listening to every cock and bull story, I'd sooner it be her than me.

I would like to make it perfectly clear, when you're in

More Questions than Answers?

a situation like this and you get no answers and are treated how I was by Lincolnshire police, it makes you very angry and bitter. Don't misunderstand, like I have said, there are lots of good police out their doing a good job, and where would we be without them? I am not condemning the police in general, I am condemning the officers that dealt with my son's case. I have relatives around the world who are police officers; one particular relative is an uncle who joined the police force in Philadelphia. It's just an experience like this, where the officers who dealt with the case didn't understand how I felt. For God's sake, what am I supposed to think?

I can never get my head around the way some of the justice is served to people; none of this is in my power. You turn the TV on and read it in the newspapers, big crimes with small sentences. I suppose it's just the way the world is today, or should I say not the world, but the people within it. Times do change, but not always for good. I read a book once where the author made a comment on how he didn't like corrupt police or people who dealt with drugs or pimps. I suppose the reality of this is in any town or city around the world

More Questions than Answers?

– it's fact, there is always going to be corruption. I hope there is always somebody watching out for them. In any profession there will always be rules broken – it's like the saying, "Rules are meant to be broken" – but it's a fact, there is no getting away from it, it happens. But what can I do? Nothing, that's up to the experts to sort out.

7

On one of my visits to a SAMM meeting I sat in a room talking to a man who had lost his son. His son was coming home from a late working shift one time, and as he was driving he noticed a car behind him, and the driver was harassing him. Eventually, when the driver had finally caught up with up him, the poor guy panicked. In doing so, he escaped from his car and, as I believe, made contact with another vehicle which contributed to his death. Some time after that he sadly passed away, having been on life support in hospital due to his injuries. I found this really sad as, again, I learned that the killers were only given light sentences, and that the charges brought were only for manslaughter.

More Questions than Answers?

With another lady whose mother had been murdered, nobody was ever been charged. You would be surprised at the stories I hear from the victims' families. The same day at the meeting a young lady turned to me and said hello, in a very polite manner. I returned the greeting and said, "Who have come here with? Your mother?" She said no. Obviously I thought she was a teenager but it turned out she was in her forties. I was amazed at how young she looked for her age. She asked me what my circumstances were, and when I explained she was very surprised at how I had handled my situation. Then I asked her what her circumstances were. She said, "I lost my son in a car accident," then paused, took a breath and then said, "Then my daughter was murdered." I just couldn't believe what I had heard! I can't imagine, she has lost two children, the poor woman. I didn't quite catch the details whether anybody had been charged, but I will find out eventually.

At these meetings there is so much to catch up on, and so many tragic circumstances. It's hard to say who has taken the biggest blows. Don't just sit there for years and bottle things up like I did, even though you should be given the advice, it does help with support. Knowing that you can relate to somebody who has gone through similar circumstances is so important – which is another reason for me writing this book. It's also been written in memory of Mark, and to convey my feelings, because after all is said and done, if somebody has never gone through similar tragic events, there is no point in trying to explain your feelings or what you go through.

I have tried explaining to people, but it's a waste of time. Some people say they can only imagine, but that's nowhere near as far as I'm concerned. People will say their mother has passed away, okay, but if they have lived to a decent age it's a natural part of life. In circumstances like losing a younger child it can't be imagined, but it's completely different situation to imagine, trust me. I don't think for one moment these people are being rude, they just don't understand. So you have to allow for that, and understand where they are coming from. Of course, some people just don't know how to approach you and say anything. Personally, if anyone ever approaches me in a polite way I'm always willing to comment – I prefer to talk

More Questions than Answers?

even though it does hurt. I know some people don't like to go on about their circumstances all the time, you have to learn to live with it, but you don't get over it. In fact, I find it to be an uphill struggle every day, so I hope this book will benefit the people. Families of victims of murder will understand – you are not on your own. I know what we go through.

I find now that I can only talk to people that have suffered similar circumstances as me. Some people I know are trying to fight against knife crime. – to change the law against knives and guns, to bring in capital punishment. I wish them all the success in doing so, because I will always be on their side. People who get reasonable justice, as I call it, still moan. Don't get me wrong, I do understand they should lock the criminals up and throw the key away. Life should mean life for murder, even capital punishment. Imagine if we in the UK had similar prisons to those in the United States. Then I think the criminals would possibly think twice before they committed these terrible crimes, especially the cold blooded, evil ones. People do say we are copying America in lots of ways; it would be nice if we dished the same punishments

More Questions than Answers?

out. Then people would feel that they have got justice. The only reason is I say, when somebody gets justice, like when I pick a newspaper up and read, for instance, about a criminal who gets sixteen years in prison for murder, and the victim's family are not happy, they wanted a bigger sentence. Then I think to myself, well okay, I do understand, I'm fully on your side, and I sympathize – but I didn't even get a trial for Mark!

Sometimes you feel you can't win – if you open your mouth and say anything you don't want to offend people, but trust me I am on your side. So really I do hope you can try to understand how I and my family feel, with the entire circumstances which surround everything. I certainly hope you realize we didn't get a fair outcome.

It doesn't matter how many words are printed in this book, somebody who has never been through these tragic ordeals will never understand, in a million years. They can laugh, joke, kid themselves and criticize, do as they like. But believe me, all this has done is turn my life and that of my family upside down, damaged for good.

More Questions than Answers?

Sometimes pieces can be picked up, as the saying goes, unfortunately not in these cases. People who don't know me often wonder why I have been so bitter towards them in certain circumstances. Well now if they have read this book they may understand the reasons why. I never put my way out to target people; I have always been fairly down to earth and laid back. I would rather help somebody genuine who is in need than make enemies. Especially now, let's face it, life is too short.

If you do meet nice people, who I know exist, it makes life a whole lot more pleasant – even though it takes all kinds to make the world go round.

8

I'm still amazed even today how people's attitudes are towards me, even though they know what I have been through. You would think they would have a heart; I have always wanted people to know this story in particular.

Going back to when I was given the news about Mark's disappearance, and told he had been murdered... at the time I was living in the south of the midlands. One day I had a call from my wife, asking me to go to Grantham to give an interview to the local paper. Having left my flat I was driving down the road, very stressed and upset, not knowing if I was coming or going. I realized I had forgotten my mobile phone and some paperwork I needed to take with me, so I decided to go back to my flat. I pulled up just outside, and I remember there being a car parked in front. Now I am always fair and reasonable in the way I park my car. Having got out and returned back to my flat to get my phone and paperwork, I thought I would make a quick cup of tea and get my act together for ten minutes, to make sure I had got everything. During this time I heard a lot of shouting and commotion outside, but I thought it was kids hanging around outside. They had been reported to the police by other neighbors for causing a nuisance. By the time I had drunk my cup of tea and walked outside, I could see two women shouting and kicking my car. I couldn't understand what the problem was, and shouted, "What are you doing?" One of the women, my upstairs neighbour, turned to me and said, "Can't you get your car close enough?" I said, "There must be at least a two feet gap, don't you think you're being a little petty? Just leave it, will you? I have enough problems without these silly things."

I don't think for one moment they were both aware of my situation at the time. It was getting quite overheated, they were both shouting and I decided to give them both as good back, word for word. I remember a neighbour across the way, who shouted to us to stop. I said, "I have done nothing wrong, why don't they just leave my car alone?" It was the last thing I needed. Anyway I told them what I thought, and drove away to Grantham and carried on with my business.

A few days later I had a visit from a police officer, who took a statement. I told him I was not causing any trouble and I didn't want any bother, just peace and quiet. He seemed to understand that I was upset with stress, and so my attitude didn't come over very well (this was a different police force to the one that was dealing with my son, not that he cared anyway). After a few days he came back again, saying there had been a problem with the hallway in the flats, claiming there had been bin bags thrown about the place. I said I knew nothing about it, which I didn't, and I said it must have been the teenagers causing trouble. He didn't believe me, and insisted it was me. I'm innocent, going through hell, and then I get treated like this, from a different police force.

More Questions than Answers?

I think the person that was making those complaints wasn't quite in a normal mental state. She was a single parent with a two month old baby, possibly suffering from post-natal depression – just an attention seeker with nothing better to do.

I decided enough was enough, so I went to the local police station and made a complaint to the sergeant about the visiting police officer, for what good it did. The sergeant said he would have a word. A few days later, it was quite nice and sunny outside, and I was stood in my kitchen, the double glazing windows opening outwards looking onto the communal garden. I took a glass of water from my tap, had a few sips then without even thinking, even though I was on a ground floor flat, just tipped the water out through the window, knowing the water wouldn't hit anybody. Unfortunately the neighbor I had had problems with about the parking and the entrance just happened to be walking past. She shouted, "Do you mind?" She called me a "dirty bastard", and said "You've just spat at me!" I tried to calm her down and told her it was water, but she was not having any of it. By this time I was fuming – I went out later that day, and she was shouting at me down the stairs from my doorway. I retaliated and gave her a piece of my mind. I can honestly say, I never spat – it was water and I never saw her. Also I never laid a finger on this person. All I wanted to do was keep the peace.

Throughout of all of this I doubt if she was even aware of my circumstances. I still think she was suffering with depression, and wanted to take her feelings out on somebody – I was just a soft target. In between I tried to make friends and get on with her; I even did her the favour of going to the next village to collect baby milk for her as she had no means of transport. I just wanted to be friendly and get on as neighbours, but it wasn't meant to be – she was just out to make trouble, an evil person.

By this time the police officer wasn't on my side as I had made a complaint against him – we didn't see eye to eye. After all, what do you expect – I wasn't in the mood for pettiness, when my son was out somewhere lying dead and all those idiots had to worry about were silly, petty, childish things. So one morning at eight o'clock, there was a loud banging on my door;

More Questions than Answers?

I looked out of my bedroom window and could see at least four police cars. I just couldn't bring to mind what the problem was, it was all happening so fast. I opened the front door and two police officers were stood in front of me. I recognized the one who had visited previously and the one that I had complained about. I didn't say a word, in fact I didn't get the chance. He said, "Get dressed, you are under arrest." I said, "Is this some sort of joke?" "No, it's no joke, get dressed we are taking you down the station," was the answer. I asked why? He said, "Just get dressed and we will tell you down at the station." I was amazed when they told me that I was being charged with harassment against the neighbour above my flat.

I decided to phone a solicitor, and gave a statement in my solicitor's presence. All the police officer did throughout the interview was be sarcastic, but I didn't bite. Even an idiot would have been able to pick up on his sarcasm. Also I know the reason for him being like this towards me was because I complained about him to his sergeant. Even though by this time he had some details about Mark, was missing and feared dead. He was cold and callous towards me, I know that.

More Questions than Answers?

I always remember last minute or two of the interview on tape, when he turned and said to me and my solicitor, "I've also taken a statement from your neighbour's sister, and she is a bank clerk. I believe everything she says because they don't lie." I turned and looked at my solicitor, who shook her head as if to say nothing. And the number of times since this I have read stories about people who work for banks who have been charged with fraud. That police officer could have decorated his living room wall with all the articles.

The state I was in after this, I had to tip-toe into my flat every night, terrified of being arrested again – and my car was vandalized. When reported it I received no feedback from the police, they were not interested. In the end I had to get away as fast as I could. I found other accommodation, the stress of it all I could have done without, all because of that evil person that caused me all the trouble. As if I wasn't going through enough torment at that time. Anyway, the police charge still stood,. I made my first appearance at Leicester Magistrate's Court, where the case was set for another date. The next hearing I had to get a note

More Questions than Answers?

from my doctor to state that I couldn't attend court to defend myself as I was not in a physical or mental state due to my circumstances. Even through all this until Mark was actually found murdered, my solicitor said, "This is disgusting, there is no way this should be taken to court." I know any normal time I could have gone and spoken, and given my side of the story in court to protest my innocence.

I also had a statement made against me from one of the neighbours who was just a nosey do-gooder who didn't understand the circumstances. Whether that would have made any difference I don't know. I think by this time they must all have known my circumstances, so where were their hearts and feelings for someone who had been told his son has been murdered? If I had done any harm to anybody then I could understand it would have been an excuse – but I hadn't laid a finger on anybody.

One morning I received a phone call from my solicitor, saying "I am sorry to tell you that I have been to court this morning on your behalf, and you have been found guilty in your absence. Also there is a warrant out for your arrest for you to appear at the magistrate's court next week, for you to be sentenced." I was totally stunned, if I had run riot or put anybody to harm or danger or threat of any nature I could understand. Imagine, all I wanted to do was grieve and get my head around the things that had happened to my son, I didn't need this petty shit.

I said to my solicitor, "Why didn't you explain my situation in detail?" He said, "I did, but they wouldn't accept it, they obviously have no sympathy." Where were my human rights? The week afterwards, I had to appear in the magistrate's court to be sentenced. As I stood in the dock, the magistrate started straight at me. It was too late, I had been found guilty, I couldn't defend myself, and I never had the chance. All I got were evil glares across the room as if I were a piece of dirt; I cannot describe how that made me feel. I will never forget that for the rest of my life, and God bless my son Mark, I hadn't even buried him yet. Not that it made any difference to any of them. I was surprised that the judge gave me a year's probation. I was numb I just couldn't speak. Thinking that I was ready to leave the court room, the magistrate said, "Hold on – for

More Questions than Answers?

the spitting you can pay £100 compensation to this lady". I just couldn't believe it. That was it, and I left the court room, and told my solicitor what I thought of him. I doubt he was much bothered anyway.

I hope it made them all happy for what they did to me. It never made me a better man, because I'm ten times a better man than any of those people, and always will be.

9

Nottingham city to me is the queen of the Midlands, but unfortunately is has a high rate in gun and knife crime. Sometimes on visits I have found it very pleasant. Over the years I have spent many times in Nottingham, at concerts, football matches and especially when Brian Clough was the manager at Nottingham Forest. I have always liked Nottingham as a city; it is a proper city with nice architecture and character. I always class it as my favorite city, but now anytime I go near Nottingham Crown Court, I have to turn my head the other way and occupy focus on something else. All the memories of the day, five suspects walked free out the main entrance, flashbacks that send me into panic, it's not pleasant. I can't blame

More Questions than Answers?

Nottingham for this, it's just sad that it happened to be one of my favorite cities where we never got justice for my son's murder, or should I say, not even a trial, let alone justice.

As I have mentioned at the start of this chapter, Mark and I once went to the Nottingham City ground in the early 1990s and had some photos taken with a few of the players. Unfortunately, one thing led to another, and we never did get the chance to go to a football match together. Mark actually told me he had never been to a football match in his life, and he always wanted to go and see Leicester City, his hometown club as he always had an interest in them. I told him we would get around to it, and I would take him sometime.

It also sickens me now to think that Mark had never been on an aeroplane in his life – there are lots of opportunities he missed out on. That's why when people in similar circumstances to me often say, "Do you ever feel guilty when you go into a shop to buy clothes, etc., go on a trip?" Then yes, you feel awful. I do think that's why a lot of times I am so hard on myself, because I have so many guilt trips. I'm told this is only natural. If there was a life sentence for Mark's killers then I am doing that sentence myself now, and I have still got the rest to do, because I have been convicted not them.

I know there is no way I will get my life back on track; I can kid myself on as much as I like, but there is no point, it's fact. I am just sitting in the dark waiting for nothing, because I know there will never be a knock on my door from somebody saying, "We have good news, you will now get a fair trial and justice.'" If the police wanted to review the case as they said, why haven't they ever sent me any information, or updated me on progress? Occasionally when I telephone Lincolnshire police, there are new arrivals who are not familiar with the case. Every time I have been to see a solicitor I am told I'm wasting my time. It's the same old story, people just want me to accept it all, grind my teeth and move on. Never in a million years will I forgive. I hate how I was treated. My question is to people who have been through similar circumstances to me. "Could you ever forgive the people that did this to your loved one ?" Ten out of ten their answer

More Questions than Answers?

is 'no'. You don't get over it'– flashbacks, memories and things that remind you, like anniversaries, birthdays and Christmas. All you can try and do is learn to live with the situation. I think that nothing will ever become of this case, in fact the harder I try the harder it gets, it's draining, physically and mentally. All I can do now is leave it to God – they say he works in mysterious ways.

Mark never deserved to be treated the way he was, it was callous and evil. Hopefully one day with God's power, who knows?

10

When I first started to write this book I doubted if I was doing the right thing, but I am glad I have now because I doubt very much we will ever get justice for Mark. That is something else I will never get over, something I will never forgive the police for. I can only try and learn to live with the situation. To them it's done, they have moved on, yes, but I will never be able to move on.

I have certainly tried to make my points clearly. There is not really a great deal more I can say. At the time when Mark had gone missing I was doing a course in photography, in which I gained qualifications and was really doing very well – practice was making me better

More Questions than Answers?

as I went along. To this day I am now classed as a professional photographer;.

I tried to keep going. One colleague who I went to college with asked me to go into business with him. Due to all the circumstances with Mark I just lost it, even to this day I have no interest. I actually loved it, bearing in mind that at that time it was only a hobby, but to do it as a full time living, I know for certain I would have done really well. I have never felt so certain about anything. I had never put time and effort into anything like that before. To this day when I last spoke to my colleague from college, he is doing very well for himself, with two photography studios. He often mentions to me I am wasting my talent as I was good, and it's a shame. But he just couldn't understand the trauma I was going through. I am so angry because I have missed out.

I'm sure there are people saying, "What if the suspects were innocent?" I agree, it did cross my mind, because I certainly wouldn't want to be charged with murder if I was innocent, and neither would anybody else in their right mind. We shall never know now, because we never

More Questions than Answers?

got a trial. I am sure the suspects would have got a fair trial, that's what trials are about – or are they? The police did say they had enough evidence against the accused, so I am sure we would have got justice, but then again, would we? I don't know – I said I hope they are all happy now laughing and joking making comments about my son. He was a human being, where were his human rights, and mine and those of my family?

What makes me angry is that the media never really said anything nice about Mark and my beliefs. Of the things they did say about him, only some were true, but it's the way they say them. Any person who sat in a room with Mark for an hour with a cup of coffee would have easily figured out he was a decent lad. I don't care what anybody thinks, I just know he was too good to be hanging around with those scum.

Given a chance, I know Mark would have been a good lad; I have come across parents in my lifetime who hate to admit their children are in the wrong, whilst knowing full well they are. They will always stick up for them, saying they are complete angels and would do no wrong. I cannot be doing with such people.

More Questions than Answers?

Mark was no angel and he had done wrong things, no way will I deny that. He was punished, but as I have said, there has to be something bigger that cost him his life, something I will never know about.

Remember that Mark had a mother and a father, sisters, brothers, uncles and aunties. All this knock-on effect, which it has brought to those people remains.

It has really hurt me over the months to put this book together, it's been far from easy, but something I have had to do. Sometimes I get so fed up putting an act on, the bravest face I can, even though inside I am hurting. The evil that took Mark away from me has denied us going to a football match, for a pint, as a father and son usually do. We had our ups and downs from time to time, but the more hurtful thing now is when I think we were getting on so well together. In hindsight, if I'd known he was in any danger I wouldn't have hesitated to do anything in my power to keep him from that danger.

Occasionally when I visit Mark's grave I just stand there, still finding it hard to imagine that it is him lying there. When I walk away I think what a waste of a young life. It is coming up to nearly ten years now, ten years of hurt. If ever there is something mentioned about Mark in a newspaper or on TV it brings it all back. My only big wish now is justice for Mark. He was born in Leicester, and went to school in Leicester after Mark's mother and I separated and she moved to Grantham. Obviously, Mark had to start a new life with his mother there, but I think maybe if she had stayed in Leicester all this would have never happened. Who knows? Either way there are always ifs and buts. People say, "You make your own luck." You get all these different comments surrounding different tragic circumstances, different categories of people who do wrong. I wouldn't want to get involved on the political side of this; it is a very complicated debate. But I don't think Mark would have done anything that bad to have contributed to his murder.

People are entitled to think what they want, and can listen to what ever stories they want, but I can only say what I believe – and I don't believe he deserved to be murdered. I suppose you could almost say it was an execution.

More Questions than Answers?

I think the government should bring back capital punishment, but we who still believe in capital punishment have got more chance of seeing it brought back than me seeing Mark and my family get a fair trial and his murderers brought to justice. I suppose I will have to dream on, as I have done for the past ten years, staring at four walls.

This is a small poem I have written for Mark.

Boy to man, I remember once when we walked through the park taking you to school. I noticed the fair was there, I thought I have no money to take you that night, I felt sad for us. I remember when you played with your toys, when we kicked ball, when we went to the seaside and when we went fishing, now all I do is think, wishing you were still here so we could both go for a beer. Yes I do cry even though I know you're still near.

More Questions than Answers?

1977   2000

MARK CORLEY 1977–2000

FROM YOUR LOVING DAD ALWAYS
TONY CORLEY